This journal belongs to:

_____

If found, return to:

_____

_____

_____

BRAVE, KIND, & Grateful

A DAILY GRATITUDE JOURNAL

by

Jessica Hische

PENGUIN WORKSHOP

Confession: I'm a terrible journaler. I'm sure many of you are very good at journaling and have experimented with every form of it. I've "experimented" with it, in that I've started and abandoned many, many journals over the years.

It always starts as a fun activity—a new book! A fancy new pen maybe! Endless possibilities! But the task quickly becomes joyless as I struggle to keep up with my high expectations of what journaling is or needs to be. I feel compelled to document every second of my day and write thoughtful and perfectly penned commentary on it—something that requires not only time but also a lot of brainpower. Time isn't something I have in spades— I have three small children, I work full-time running my own design and lettering studio, and I'm the "CEO" and "CFO" and "General Manager" of our household. You probably feel equally stretched thin most days—we are busy humans! When I do have time to myself, I'm so tired that I'm much more likely to zonk out to an episode of reality TV than I am to sit down and write thoughtful reflections from my day.

But this is the magic of gratitude journaling! It only takes a few minutes per day, and there are useful prompts to help you put pen to paper . . . even when you feel like a zombie. By setting aside a few minutes each day to write down and reflect on what I'm grateful for, I feel energized and renewed. It keeps me centered, it allows me to be hopeful, and it reinforces the love that I am surrounded by every day.

Above all, gratitude journaling is a tool, and I love making tools to help others. Every time I pick up a new skill or discover a better way to navigate whatever life throws at me, I'm inspired to pass on that knowledge through writing, design, or art. For *Tomorrow I'll Be Brave* and *Tomorrow I'll Be Kind*, my first two kids books, I was inspired to share life skills with little ones—seemingly simple behaviors and mindsets that even some grown-ups have a difficult time grasping. *Tomorrow I'll Be Brave* teaches the importance of forgiving yourself if you don't achieve your goals—that there's always tomorrow to try again. *Tomorrow I'll Be Kind* talks about how even super small acts of kindness can have a huge impact on people's lives.

I've talked a lot about how these two books work together—how *Brave*'s missions of courage and forgiveness fuel our ability to help those around us . . . something you learn all about in *Kind*. My hope is that this journal helps you further explore this simple, necessary act of self-discovery. Gratitude journaling might seem like something you're doing all for yourself, but the positive changes you'll see in your own life will ripple out into the world. Gratitude is a peace bringer, a love and joy multiplier, and so many other things we'll talk about in this book. I'm personally grateful that you're joining me and trusting me on your gratitude journey, and I can't wait for you to experience all the wonderful things a gratitude practice can bring to your life.

How it works...

Begin each day with a few minutes of gratitude for anything or anyone, and a pledge to express gratitude to something or someone.

Date: __4__ / __27__

Three things I'm grateful for today:

1. THE CRAZY GOOD PASTRIES FROM my LOCAL COFFEE SHOP

2. THE MEMORY OF my FAMILY at GRANDMA'S SUMMER TRAILER

3. THE FLOWERS IN my yard THAT BRING HUMMINGBIRDS ALL year LONG

Today I'll express my gratitude to:

MY FRIEND FROM COLLEGE WHO I HAVEN'T TALKED TO IN A WHILE BUT LOVE & MISS SO MUCH!

Take five slow, deep breaths. Inhale and exhale in gratitude.

End each evening with a reflection on the things that brought you light and happiness—as well as an invitation to set a mini goal for yourself for the day ahead.

Three small moments of joy I experienced today:

1. I MADE A PERFECT PANCAKE!
FINALLY FIGURED OUT THAT RECIPE.

2. I RAN INTO ERIC AT THE CORNER STORE
AND IT WAS SO GREAT TO CATCH UP.

3. I TOOK OFF WORK A LITTLE EARLY TO
TAKE RAMONA OUT FOR ICE CREAM.

Tomorrow I'll do my best to:

TAKE A WALK AROUND THE LAKE IN
THE AFTERNOON IF I'M FEELING STRESSED
ABOUT WORK.

Take five slow, deep breaths. Reflect in gratitude.

When I was a kid, I had a hard time getting excited about new activities. I hated being "bad at stuff." I only wanted to do things I easily excelled at (art) and avoided anything I didn't have a natural talent for (any sport that involved running). I was really hard on myself when I "messed up" or didn't get things right the first time around. Even when I did accomplish something, I couldn't enjoy or appreciate the path it took to get there because I was so focused on success. It wasn't until later that I realized how important failure is for personal growth. That you can be mediocre (or even terrible) at something and still enjoy doing it. Kurt Vonnegut said it best—"Being good at things isn't the point of doing them."

The same can be said for your gratitude practice. The path toward gratitude is ever-changing, relentless, and let's be honest, extremely challenging. But the fact of the matter is, you don't have to be good at it! You just have to try. That is where success lies—in the monumental decisions we make every day to just simply try.

Every journey begins with a first step.
Make the commitment to follow through
as best you can—and forgive yourself if
you have to pause and take a breath.

I, _____ , promise to find a few moments each day to pause and reflect on the good things and people in my life.

~~~~~~~~

Date: ___/___   _____

I'm *always* grateful for . . .

When you start thinking about what you're grateful for, there are probably a handful of people and things that are always top of mind. Take a moment to write some of them down so you can let yourself off the hook for listing them every day.

1. _____

2. _____

3. _____

4. _____

5. _____

6. _____

7. _____

8. _____

9. _____

10. _____

Date: ___/___

Three things I'm grateful for today:

1. _____

_____

2. _____

_____

3. _____

_____

Today I'll express my gratitude to:

Take five slow, deep breaths. Inhale and exhale in gratitude.

Three small moments of joy I experienced today:

1. _____

_____

2. _____

_____

3. _____

_____

Tomorrow I'll do my best to:

Take five slow, deep breaths. Reflect in gratitude.

Date: ___/___  _____

Three things I'm grateful for today:

1. _____

_____

2. _____

_____

3. _____

_____

Today I'll express my gratitude to:

Take five slow, deep breaths. Inhale and exhale in gratitude.

Three small moments of joy I experienced today:

1. _____

_____

2. _____

_____

3. _____

_____

Tomorrow I'll do my best to:

Take five slow, deep breaths. Reflect in gratitude.

Date: ____ / ____   _____

Three things I'm grateful for today:

1. _____

_____

2. _____

_____

3. _____

_____

Today I'll express my gratitude to:

Take five slow, deep breaths. Inhale and exhale in gratitude.

Three small moments of joy I experienced today:

1. _____

_____

2. _____

_____

3. _____

_____

Tomorrow I'll do my best to:

Take five slow, deep breaths. Reflect in gratitude.

Date: ____ / ____

Three things I'm grateful for today:

1. _____

_____

2. _____

_____

3. _____

_____

Today I'll express my gratitude to:

Take five slow, deep breaths. Inhale and exhale in gratitude.

Three small moments of joy I experienced today:

1. _____

_____

2. _____

_____

3. _____

_____

Tomorrow I'll do my best to:

Take five slow, deep breaths. Reflect in gratitude.

Date: ___ / ___

Three things I'm grateful for today:

1. _____

_____

2. _____

_____

3. _____

_____

Today I'll express my gratitude to:

Take five slow, deep breaths. Inhale and exhale in gratitude.

Three small moments of joy I experienced today:

1. _____

_____

2. _____

_____

3. _____

_____

Tomorrow I'll do my best to:

Take five slow, deep breaths. Reflect in gratitude.

Date: _____ / _____

Three things I'm grateful for today:

1. _____

_____

2. _____

_____

3. _____

_____

Today I'll express my gratitude to:

Take five slow, deep breaths. Inhale and exhale in gratitude.

Three small moments of joy I experienced today:

1. _____

_____

2. _____

_____

3. _____

_____

Tomorrow I'll do my best to:

Take five slow, deep breaths. Reflect in gratitude.

Date: ____ / ____  _____

Three things I'm grateful for today:

1. _____

_____

2. _____

_____

3. _____

_____

Today I'll express my gratitude to:

Take five slow, deep breaths. Inhale and exhale in gratitude.

Three small moments of joy I experienced today:

1. _____

_____

2. _____

_____

3. _____

_____

Tomorrow I'll do my best to:

Take five slow, deep breaths. Reflect in gratitude.

Gratitude TAKES PRACTICE

When I was in my early twenties, I knew I wanted to make illustrating letters a part of my daily life. After scheming a bunch of different ways to make it happen, I finally settled on a method that stuck—I would draw a single letter every day with the goal of working through the alphabet twelve times (an arbitrary number, but it seemed both ambitious and doable). For a year and a half, my day began with this creative exercise. I gave myself some parameters (work on each letter for a half hour tops) and made myself accountable to others (I shared them every day online). And while I definitely did skip a few days for one reason or another, the amount of good that routine brought to my life has been immeasurable.

The beautiful thing about a daily gratitude practice is that it is exactly that: a practice. Setting aside just a few minutes every day to breathe and feel truly present can have an incredible impact on how you experience your life. The more consistently you carve out time to feel grateful, the deeper your gratitude will be.

If not now . . .

Is there a time in the morning that you can carve out to feel gratitude? How about in the evening? Write them down here:

_____ : ____ a.m.

_____ : ____ p.m.

What are some other moments throughout the day that are more often taken over by mindless internetting and can instead be filled with thoughts or actions of gratitude?

The ABCs of Gratitude

A Nighttime Exercise

~~~~~~~~~~~~~~~

Sometimes I find myself spinning out at bedtime, thinking about what I could have done better that day or worrying about the difficulties awaiting me tomorrow. In those moments, I find it hard to be present in my body or even in my bedroom—my mind is everywhere but resting peacefully on my pillow.

I was asking a friend about what she does to manage those nighttime anxious thoughts and she told me of a wonderful tool called The ABCs of Gratitude. Instead of "counting sheep," you work your way one letter at a time through the alphabet—naming something you're grateful for that starts with that letter. You don't have to overthink it; it can be the first thing that pops into your head, but for each item or person, pause for a moment to reflect and feel truly grateful. Even if you've listed "Apples" for *A*, you might find yourself thinking of a happy memory from your life—for me, apple picking with friends in upstate New York after spending a long peaceful train ride staring at beautiful fall foliage in the Hudson Valley.

List some of your favorite items by letter here, or just use this activity as part of your gratitude practice.

A _____

B _____

C _____

D _____

E _____

F _____

G _____

H _____

I _____

J _____

K _____

L _____

M _____

N _____

O _____

P _____

Q _____

R _____

S _____

T _____

U _____

V _____

W _____

X _____

Y _____

Z _____

Date: ____ / ____

Three things I'm grateful for today:

1. _____

_____

2. _____

_____

3. _____

_____

Today I'll express my gratitude to:

Take five slow, deep breaths. Inhale and exhale in gratitude.

Three small moments of joy I experienced today:

1. _____

_____

2. _____

_____

3. _____

_____

Tomorrow I'll do my best to:

Take five slow, deep breaths. Reflect in gratitude.

Date: _____ / _____

Three things I'm grateful for today:

1. _____

_____

2. _____

_____

3. _____

_____

Today I'll express my gratitude to:

Take five slow, deep breaths. Inhale and exhale in gratitude.

Three small moments of joy I experienced today:

1. _____

_____

2. _____

_____

3. _____

_____

Tomorrow I'll do my best to:

Take five slow, deep breaths. Reflect in gratitude.

Date: ___/___

Three things I'm grateful for today:

1. _____

_____

2. _____

_____

3. _____

_____

Today I'll express my gratitude to:

Take five slow, deep breaths. Inhale and exhale in gratitude.

Three small moments of joy I experienced today:

1. _____

_____

2. _____

_____

3. _____

_____

Tomorrow I'll do my best to:

Take five slow, deep breaths. Reflect in gratitude.

Date: ____ / ____    _____

Three things I'm grateful for today:

1. _____

_____

2. _____

_____

3. _____

_____

Today I'll express my gratitude to:

Take five slow, deep breaths. Inhale and exhale in gratitude.

Three small moments of joy I experienced today:

1. _____

_____

2. _____

_____

3. _____

_____

Tomorrow I'll do my best to:

Take five slow, deep breaths. Reflect in gratitude.

Date: ___/___

Three things I'm grateful for today:

1. _____

_____

2. _____

_____

3. _____

_____

Today I'll express my gratitude to:

Take five slow, deep breaths. Inhale and exhale in gratitude.

Three small moments of joy I experienced today:

1. _____

_____

2. _____

_____

3. _____

_____

Tomorrow I'll do my best to:

Take five slow, deep breaths. Reflect in gratitude.

Date: ____ / ____

Three things I'm grateful for today:

1. _____

_____

2. _____

_____

3. _____

_____

Today I'll express my gratitude to:

Take five slow, deep breaths. Inhale and exhale in gratitude.

Three small moments of joy I experienced today:

1. _____

_____

2. _____

_____

3. _____

_____

Tomorrow I'll do my best to:

Take five slow, deep breaths. Reflect in gratitude.

Date: _____ / _____

Three things I'm grateful for today:

1. _____

_____

2. _____

_____

3. _____

_____

Today I'll express my gratitude to:

Take five slow, deep breaths. Inhale and exhale in gratitude.

Three small moments of joy I experienced today:

1. _____

_____

2. _____

_____

3. _____

_____

Tomorrow I'll do my best to:

Take five slow, deep breaths. Reflect in gratitude.

One morning as I was getting ready for work, I saw my five-year-old standing in front of the full-length mirror in my bedroom. She was quiet, and I asked what was on her mind. Her answer broke my heart. She said, "I wish I had a different and more beautiful face."

I struggled with body image issues as a teen (I hate that I can still analyze the caloric content of food somewhat accurately), so I've made a real effort to never talk about myself negatively in front of her and do my best to shield her from media that might undermine messages of body positivity. The incident inspired a good conversation between her and me, and also an art piece: I drew the phrase "You Are Enough" and laser cut it as a mirror. When I posted an image online, the response was overwhelming. I heard from hundreds of people about how deeply it resonated.

Practicing self-love is a lifelong process—a tough one, but such a worthy one. It's also one of the ultimate expressions of gratitude for yourself and for others. Accepting and appreciating who you are has a funny way of also rubbing off on those around you. Understanding that we are all flawed, but also beautiful and unique and worthy of love is gratitude at work.

Love yourself so you can reflect love back to the world.

What are ten things that you love about yourself? Or ten unique qualities that you want to develop a deeper appreciation for?

1. _____

2. _____

3. _____

4. _____

5. _____

6. _____

7. _____

8. _____

9. _____

10. _____

Date: ____/____

Three things I'm grateful for today:

1. _____

_____

2. _____

_____

3. _____

_____

Today I'll express my gratitude to:

Take five slow, deep breaths. Inhale and exhale in gratitude.

Three small moments of joy I experienced today:

1. _____

_____

2. _____

_____

3. _____

_____

Tomorrow I'll do my best to:

Take five slow, deep breaths. Reflect in gratitude.

Date: ____ / ____

Three things I'm grateful for today:

1. _____

_____

2. _____

_____

3. _____

_____

Today I'll express my gratitude to:

Take five slow, deep breaths. Inhale and exhale in gratitude.

Three small moments of joy I experienced today:

1. _____

_____

2. _____

_____

3. _____

_____

Tomorrow I'll do my best to:

Take five slow, deep breaths. Reflect in gratitude.

Date: ____ / ____

Three things I'm grateful for today:

1. _____

_____

2. _____

_____

3. _____

_____

Today I'll express my gratitude to:

Take five slow, deep breaths. Inhale and exhale in gratitude.

Three small moments of joy I experienced today:

1. _____

_____

2. _____

_____

3. _____

_____

Tomorrow I'll do my best to:

Take five slow, deep breaths. Reflect in gratitude.

57

Date: ___ / ___

Three things I'm grateful for today:

1. _____

_____

2. _____

_____

3. _____

_____

Today I'll express my gratitude to:

Take five slow, deep breaths. Inhale and exhale in gratitude.

Three small moments of joy I experienced today:

1. _____

_____

2. _____

_____

3. _____

_____

Tomorrow I'll do my best to:

Take five slow, deep breaths. Reflect in gratitude.

Date: ___/___

Three things I'm grateful for today:

1. _____

_____

2. _____

_____

3. _____

_____

Today I'll express my gratitude to:

Take five slow, deep breaths. Inhale and exhale in gratitude.

Three small moments of joy I experienced today:

1. _____

_____

2. _____

_____

3. _____

_____

Tomorrow I'll do my best to:

Take five slow, deep breaths. Reflect in gratitude.

Date: ___ / ___

Three things I'm grateful for today:

1. _____

_____

2. _____

_____

3. _____

_____

Today I'll express my gratitude to:

Take five slow, deep breaths. Inhale and exhale in gratitude.

Three small moments of joy I experienced today:

1. _____
_____

2. _____
_____

3. _____
_____

Tomorrow I'll do my best to:

Take five slow, deep breaths. Reflect in gratitude.

Date: ___ / ___

Three things I'm grateful for today:

1. _____

_____

2. _____

_____

3. _____

_____

Today I'll express my gratitude to:

Take five slow, deep breaths. Inhale and exhale in gratitude.

Three small moments of joy I experienced today:

1. _____

_____

2. _____

_____

3. _____

_____

Tomorrow I'll do my best to:

Take five slow, deep breaths. Reflect in gratitude.

Gratitude FOSTERS HUMILITY

Several years ago, I got an email that I couldn't have ever dreamed of receiving—I was being asked to design the title font for Wes Anderson's *Moonrise Kingdom*. I had always been such a big fan of his movies, and after nearly exploding from excitement, I immediately said yes. Over the course of the next few months, I worked with Wes to bring the *Moonrise Kingdom* titles to life. The project came at a time when I was feeling a little grumbly about work—I had a few projects go sideways back-to-back, and my relationships with clients were feeling more adversarial than cooperative.

Working with Wes was such a breath of fresh air. I walked into critiques with an open heart and viewed the process as dialogue between his mind and my hands. Through this process, I realized how big of an impact gratitude and humility can have on my work. Other clients weren't being "difficult"—I just hadn't trusted them. They had hired me for my expertise, but I didn't understand that they were experts, too (they know way more about their businesses than I do!), and we could combine our expertise to make magic.

I realized that if I walked into every project with the same enthusiasm, trust, and humility that I did at the start of *Moonrise Kingdom*, not only would my work be way better but my relationships would be better, too.

Just happy to be here . . .

What are some things you hope to learn or get better at this year? What can you do to feel some of that "I'm just happy to be here" magic every day?

Take five slow, deep breaths. Reflect in gratitude.

Date: ____ / ____

Three things I'm grateful for today:

1. _____

_____

2. _____

_____

3. _____

_____

Today I'll express my gratitude to:

Take five slow, deep breaths. Inhale and exhale in gratitude.

Three small moments of joy I experienced today:

1. _____

_____

2. _____

_____

3. _____

_____

Tomorrow I'll do my best to:

Take five slow, deep breaths. Reflect in gratitude.

Date: ___ / ___

Three things I'm grateful for today:

1. _____

_____

2. _____

_____

3. _____

_____

Today I'll express my gratitude to:

Take five slow, deep breaths. Inhale and exhale in gratitude.

Three small moments of joy I experienced today:

1. _____
_____

2. _____
_____

3. _____
_____

Tomorrow I'll do my best to:

Take five slow, deep breaths. Reflect in gratitude.

Date: ____/____

Three things I'm grateful for today:

1. _____

_____

2. _____

_____

3. _____

_____

Today I'll express my gratitude to:

Take five slow, deep breaths. Inhale and exhale in gratitude.

Three small moments of joy I experienced today:

1. _____

_____

2. _____

_____

3. _____

_____

Tomorrow I'll do my best to:

Take five slow, deep breaths. Reflect in gratitude.

Date: ____ / ____

Three things I'm grateful for today:

1. _____

_____

2. _____

_____

3. _____

_____

Today I'll express my gratitude to:

Take five slow, deep breaths. Inhale and exhale in gratitude.

Three small moments of joy I experienced today:

1. _____

_____

2. _____

_____

3. _____

_____

Tomorrow I'll do my best to:

Take five slow, deep breaths. Reflect in gratitude.

Date: ____ / ____

Three things I'm grateful for today:

1. _____

_____

2. _____

_____

3. _____

_____

Today I'll express my gratitude to:

Take five slow, deep breaths. Inhale and exhale in gratitude.

Three small moments of joy I experienced today:

1. _____

_____

2. _____

_____

3. _____

_____

Tomorrow I'll do my best to:

Take five slow, deep breaths. Reflect in gratitude.

Date: ___/___    _____

Three things I'm grateful for today:

1. _____

_____

2. _____

_____

3. _____

_____

Today I'll express my gratitude to:

Take five slow, deep breaths. Inhale and exhale in gratitude.

Three small moments of joy I experienced today:

1. _____

_____

2. _____

_____

3. _____

_____

Tomorrow I'll do my best to:

Take five slow, deep breaths. Reflect in gratitude.

Date: _____ / _____

Three things I'm grateful for today:

1. _____

_____

2. _____

_____

3. _____

_____

Today I'll express my gratitude to:

Take five slow, deep breaths. Inhale and exhale in gratitude.

Three small moments of joy I experienced today:

1. _____

_____

2. _____

_____

3. _____

_____

Tomorrow I'll do my best to:

Take five slow, deep breaths. Reflect in gratitude.

All of us have helpers in our lives—people who, in small ways or in big ways, lift us up. They help us because they care about us, but also because they probably remember a time when they were in our shoes and the gratitude they felt for the people who helped them. I've been so incredibly lucky to have supportive people around me and mentors who have opened doors for me professionally. The gratitude I feel for them fuels me and makes me want to help others. It inspires me to pass down knowledge to artists earlier in their careers, either directly through one-on-one mentorship or indirectly by creating resources for them that I wish existed when I was starting out. Either way, it's sparked because of the gratitude I feel for my life and for those who've helped me.

Empathy is infectious.

Write about three times in your life when a helper made your day brighter in a big or small way.

1. _____

_____

2. _____

_____

3. _____

_____

How can you take your gratitude for one of these moments and use it to help others?

Date: ___ / ___

Three things I'm grateful for today:

1. _____

_____

2. _____

_____

3. _____

_____

Today I'll express my gratitude to:

Take five slow, deep breaths. Inhale and exhale in gratitude.

Three small moments of joy I experienced today:

1. _____

_____

2. _____

_____

3. _____

_____

Tomorrow I'll do my best to:

Take five slow, deep breaths. Reflect in gratitude.

Date: ____ / ____

Three things I'm grateful for today:

1. _____

_____

2. _____

_____

3. _____

_____

Today I'll express my gratitude to:

Take five slow, deep breaths. Inhale and exhale in gratitude.

Three small moments of joy I experienced today:

1. _____

_____

2. _____

_____

3. _____

_____

Tomorrow I'll do my best to:

Take five slow, deep breaths. Reflect in gratitude.

Date: _____ / _____

Three things I'm grateful for today:

1. _____

_____

2. _____

_____

3. _____

_____

Today I'll express my gratitude to:

Take five slow, deep breaths. Inhale and exhale in gratitude.

Three small moments of joy I experienced today:

1. _____

_____

2. _____

_____

3. _____

_____

Tomorrow I'll do my best to:

Take five slow, deep breaths. Reflect in gratitude.

Date: ____ / ____

Three things I'm grateful for today:

1. _____

_____

2. _____

_____

3. _____

_____

Today I'll express my gratitude to:

Take five slow, deep breaths. Inhale and exhale in gratitude.

Three small moments of joy I experienced today:

1. _____

_____

2. _____

_____

3. _____

_____

Tomorrow I'll do my best to:

Take five slow, deep breaths. Reflect in gratitude.

Date: ____ / ____

Three things I'm grateful for today:

1. _____

_____

2. _____

_____

3. _____

_____

Today I'll express my gratitude to:

Take five slow, deep breaths. Inhale and exhale in gratitude.

Three small moments of joy I experienced today:

1. _____

_____

2. _____

_____

3. _____

_____

Tomorrow I'll do my best to:

Take five slow, deep breaths. Reflect in gratitude.

Date: ___ / ___

Three things I'm grateful for today:

1. _____

_____

2. _____

_____

3. _____

_____

Today I'll express my gratitude to:

Take five slow, deep breaths. Inhale and exhale in gratitude.

Three small moments of joy I experienced today:

1. _____

_____

2. _____

_____

3. _____

_____

Tomorrow I'll do my best to:

Take five slow, deep breaths. Reflect in gratitude.

Date: ___ / ___

Three things I'm grateful for today:

1. _____

_____

2. _____

_____

3. _____

_____

Today I'll express my gratitude to:

Take five slow, deep breaths. Inhale and exhale in gratitude.

Three small moments of joy I experienced today:

1. _____

_____

2. _____

_____

3. _____

_____

Tomorrow I'll do my best to:

Take five slow, deep breaths. Reflect in gratitude.

When we think about what "peace" means, it's hard not to define what it is by what it isn't—war, friction, unease. When we seek peace, we're usually seeking an end to one of those not-so-great things. But we can find peace even when everything isn't going right—even when there's still lots of stuff to worry about, a conflict we can't really resolve, or a hardship we might never fully overcome. That's where gratitude steps in.

When I was fourteen, my parents got divorced, and the years that followed shaped who I am in profound ways. It was totally destabilizing—at times even traumatizing—but I'm grateful for it. It made me so much stronger, so much more independent. It taught me how to advocate for myself and showed me how much my words and actions matter. Twenty years later, it still deeply impacts my family, but it no longer feels like a massive weight on my shoulders. We continue to work through it together and show up for one another. Our relationships aren't always free of conflict (whose are?), but my gratitude for how far we've come and what I've learned from it all overshadows everything else.

The path to peace is filled with bumps and road blocks . . .

What is something you've struggled to overcome?

How can you take time to celebrate what you have learned and accomplished as you've worked to overcome it?

Date: ____ / ____

Three things I'm grateful for today:

1. _____

_____

2. _____

_____

3. _____

_____

Today I'll express my gratitude to:

Take five slow, deep breaths. Inhale and exhale in gratitude.

Three small moments of joy I experienced today:

1. _____

_____

2. _____

_____

3. _____

_____

Tomorrow I'll do my best to:

Take five slow, deep breaths. Reflect in gratitude.

Date: ___ / ___

Three things I'm grateful for today:

1. _____

_____

2. _____

_____

3. _____

_____

Today I'll express my gratitude to:

Take five slow, deep breaths. Inhale and exhale in gratitude.

Three small moments of joy I experienced today:

1. _____

_____

2. _____

_____

3. _____

_____

Tomorrow I'll do my best to:

Take five slow, deep breaths. Reflect in gratitude.

Date: ____ / ____

Three things I'm grateful for today:

1. _____

_____

2. _____

_____

3. _____

_____

Today I'll express my gratitude to:

Take five slow, deep breaths. Inhale and exhale in gratitude.

Three small moments of joy I experienced today:

1. _____

_____

2. _____

_____

3. _____

_____

Tomorrow I'll do my best to:

Take five slow, deep breaths. Reflect in gratitude.

Date: ____ / ____

Three things I'm grateful for today:

1. _____

_____

2. _____

_____

3. _____

_____

Today I'll express my gratitude to:

Take five slow, deep breaths. Inhale and exhale in gratitude.

Three small moments of joy I experienced today:

1. _____

_____

2. _____

_____

3. _____

_____

Tomorrow I'll do my best to:

Take five slow, deep breaths. Reflect in gratitude.

Date: ____ / ____ _____

Three things I'm grateful for today:

1. _____

_____

2. _____

_____

3. _____

_____

Today I'll express my gratitude to:

Take five slow, deep breaths. Inhale and exhale in gratitude.

Three small moments of joy I experienced today:

1. _____

_____

2. _____

_____

3. _____

_____

Tomorrow I'll do my best to:

Take five slow, deep breaths. Reflect in gratitude.

Date: ____ / ____

Three things I'm grateful for today:

1. _____

_____

2. _____

_____

3. _____

_____

Today I'll express my gratitude to:

Take five slow, deep breaths. Inhale and exhale in gratitude.

Three small moments of joy I experienced today:

1. _____

_____

2. _____

_____

3. _____

_____

Tomorrow I'll do my best to:

Take five slow, deep breaths. Reflect in gratitude.

Date: ____ / ____

Three things I'm grateful for today:

1. _____

_____

2. _____

_____

3. _____

_____

Today I'll express my gratitude to:

Take five slow, deep breaths. Inhale and exhale in gratitude.

Three small moments of joy I experienced today:

1. _____

_____

2. _____

_____

3. _____

_____

Tomorrow I'll do my best to:

Take five slow, deep breaths. Reflect in gratitude.

Gratitude SPARKS JOY

've lived in Northern California for the better part of a decade now. I love it here, but I'm an East Coaster at heart—raised in the snowy Poconos of Pennsylvania. As a kid, northeastern winters felt so oppressive. Yes, it was fun to go sledding and build snow forts, but every year, we'd be in school until nearly July making up for missed snow days. When we first moved to California, I was so happy to say goodbye to winter forever, but over time I started missing the dramatic seasonal shifts.

One of my clearest and most joyful memories from childhood was on a beautiful spring day following a particularly harsh winter. I was probably eleven or twelve. I put on shorts for the first time after the better part of a year and took my bike out for a ride. We lived about two miles from town, and this was the first time I was given permission to ride beyond the borders of our neighborhood. As I pedaled alone down the hilly rural roads, through endless beautiful farmland, I could feel the still-crisp air on my bare legs and the sun on my face. It was absolutely euphoric.

I love that memory because it reminds me that the happiest moments of our lives are often the simplest ones—the times when we've felt alive in our bodies and physically connected to the world around us. It also reminds me to be grateful for the difficult times, because without winter, that spring day wouldn't have been half as magical.

Little moments of magic . . .

Share a joyful memory from the past week, month, or year—
something small and beautiful that made you feel happy to be alive.

Take five slow, deep breaths. Reflect in gratitude.

Date: ____ / ____

Three things I'm grateful for today:

1. _____

_____

2. _____

_____

3. _____

_____

Today I'll express my gratitude to:

Take five slow, deep breaths. Inhale and exhale in gratitude.

Three small moments of joy I experienced today:

1. _____

_____

2. _____

_____

3. _____

_____

Tomorrow I'll do my best to:

Take five slow, deep breaths. Reflect in gratitude.

Date: ___ / ___

Three things I'm grateful for today:

1. _____

_____

2. _____

_____

3. _____

_____

Today I'll express my gratitude to:

Take five slow, deep breaths. Inhale and exhale in gratitude.

Three small moments of joy I experienced today:

1. _____

_____

2. _____

_____

3. _____

_____

Tomorrow I'll do my best to:

Take five slow, deep breaths. Reflect in gratitude.

Date: ___/___

Three things I'm grateful for today:

1. _____

_____

2. _____

_____

3. _____

_____

Today I'll express my gratitude to:

Take five slow, deep breaths. Inhale and exhale in gratitude.

Three small moments of joy I experienced today:

1. _____

_____

2. _____

_____

3. _____

_____

Tomorrow I'll do my best to:

Take five slow, deep breaths. Reflect in gratitude.

Date: ____ / ____

Three things I'm grateful for today:

1. _____

_____

2. _____

_____

3. _____

_____

Today I'll express my gratitude to:

Take five slow, deep breaths. Inhale and exhale in gratitude.

Three small moments of joy I experienced today:

1. _____

_____

2. _____

_____

3. _____

_____

Tomorrow I'll do my best to:

Take five slow, deep breaths. Reflect in gratitude.

Date: ____/____

Three things I'm grateful for today:

1. _____

_____

2. _____

_____

3. _____

_____

Today I'll express my gratitude to:

Take five slow, deep breaths. Inhale and exhale in gratitude.

Three small moments of joy I experienced today:

1. _____

_____

2. _____

_____

3. _____

_____

Tomorrow I'll do my best to:

Take five slow, deep breaths. Reflect in gratitude.

Date: ____ / ____

Three things I'm grateful for today:

1. _____

_____

2. _____

_____

3. _____

_____

Today I'll express my gratitude to:

Take five slow, deep breaths. Inhale and exhale in gratitude.

Three small moments of joy I experienced today:

1. _____

_____

2. _____

_____

3. _____

_____

Tomorrow I'll do my best to:

Take five slow, deep breaths. Reflect in gratitude.

Date: _____ / _____

Three things I'm grateful for today:

1. _____

_____

2. _____

_____

3. _____

_____

Today I'll express my gratitude to:

Take five slow, deep breaths. Inhale and exhale in gratitude.

Three small moments of joy I experienced today:

1. _____

_____

2. _____

_____

3. _____

_____

Tomorrow I'll do my best to:

Take five slow, deep breaths. Reflect in gratitude.

My brother and I are very different people. I was the art kid, and he was the sports kid. I was the sensitive feeler, and he was the brash smart aleck. I'm a hopeless optimist, and he's a realist / occasional pessimist. I'm a married mother of three who lives in a big city, and he's a single guy who lives in a small town.

Despite our differences, we were very close as kids. Having a sibling to play with, especially on those countless snow days, was wonderful. But as we got older, our relationship shifted. We spent less time together as teenagers and even less after college. We barely spoke on the phone and saw each other maybe once a year. For a while I thought that our closeness as kids was entirely due to proximity, and since we lived on opposite ends of the country, I couldn't hope to get that closeness back.

I never thought of my brother as a "family guy"—he hated family gatherings when we were growing up and, for a while, was a self-proclaimed "lifetime bachelor." But when I had my first child, he immediately dove into the role of "Uncle Matt." Seeing him interact with my kids, how much he clearly enjoys spending time with them, and how tuned in he is when they're together fills me with such a deep love and gratitude for him. I feel lucky that my kids can grow up with an uncle that cares about them so much, and that gratitude I feel has deepened my love for him. It's made me want to be a better sister, to try harder to be in each other's lives, and to let him know how much I appreciate him.

Psst, I've gotta tell you something . . .

Name someone you are grateful for who may not know it:

_____

What are five things you love about that person?

1. _____

2. _____

3. _____

4. _____

5. _____

How will you show your appreciation for them this week?

Date: ____ / ____

Three things I'm grateful for today:

1. _____

_____

2. _____

_____

3. _____

_____

Today I'll express my gratitude to:

Take five slow, deep breaths. Inhale and exhale in gratitude.

Three small moments of joy I experienced today:

1. _____

_____

2. _____

_____

3. _____

_____

Tomorrow I'll do my best to:

Take five slow, deep breaths. Reflect in gratitude.

Date: ____ / ____

Three things I'm grateful for today:

1. _____

_____

2. _____

_____

3. _____

_____

Today I'll express my gratitude to:

Take five slow, deep breaths. Inhale and exhale in gratitude.

Three small moments of joy I experienced today:

1. _____

_____

2. _____

_____

3. _____

_____

Tomorrow I'll do my best to:

Take five slow, deep breaths. Reflect in gratitude.

Date: ___/___

Three things I'm grateful for today:

1. _____

_____

2. _____

_____

3. _____

_____

Today I'll express my gratitude to:

Take five slow, deep breaths. Inhale and exhale in gratitude.

Three small moments of joy I experienced today:

1. _____

_____

2. _____

_____

3. _____

_____

Tomorrow I'll do my best to:

Take five slow, deep breaths. Reflect in gratitude.

Date: ____ / ____

Three things I'm grateful for today:

1. _____

_____

2. _____

_____

3. _____

_____

Today I'll express my gratitude to:

Take five slow, deep breaths. Inhale and exhale in gratitude.

Three small moments of joy I experienced today:

1. _____

_____

2. _____

_____

3. _____

_____

Tomorrow I'll do my best to:

Take five slow, deep breaths. Reflect in gratitude.

Date: ____/____

Three things I'm grateful for today:

1. _____

_____

2. _____

_____

3. _____

_____

Today I'll express my gratitude to:

Take five slow, deep breaths. Inhale and exhale in gratitude.

Three small moments of joy I experienced today:

1. _____

_____

2. _____

_____

3. _____

_____

Tomorrow I'll do my best to:

Take five slow, deep breaths. Reflect in gratitude.

Date: ___/___

Three things I'm grateful for today:

1. _____

_____

2. _____

_____

3. _____

_____

Today I'll express my gratitude to:

Take five slow, deep breaths. Inhale and exhale in gratitude.

Three small moments of joy I experienced today:

1. _____

_____

2. _____

_____

3. _____

_____

Tomorrow I'll do my best to:

Take five slow, deep breaths. Reflect in gratitude.

Date: ____ / ____

Three things I'm grateful for today:

1. _____

_____

2. _____

_____

3. _____

_____

Today I'll express my gratitude to:

Take five slow, deep breaths. Inhale and exhale in gratitude.

Three small moments of joy I experienced today:

1. _____

_____

2. _____

_____

3. _____

_____

Tomorrow I'll do my best to:

Take five slow, deep breaths. Reflect in gratitude.

Gratitude
RESTORES
POWER

For my entire life I've been a "feeler." I was a "very sensitive" little kid—my feelings were easily hurt, and I got wicked secondhand embarrassment for characters on TV. I hated it at the time. I wished I was more resilient, that I cared less about what others thought, and that I could coast through life without a care in the world.

Vulnerability and empathy can feel like a weakness, but it's actually an incredible strength. It took me a while to realize that, in fact, it's actually my superpower. And I'm so unbelievably grateful for it. Having a "hyperactive empathy muscle" means I truly love meeting new people and can feel a deep connection to them quickly. It also helps me make decisions about my work, particularly my online shop—I can clearly visualize the audience for things I create and can feel the excitement they'll have when receiving a piece of my art.

We all have unique superpowers, and sometimes what we perceive as a weakness is actually a strength we haven't figured out how to best utilize yet.

What are your superpowers?

What are your strengths? What are your weaknesses? How can you work to view "weaknesses" in a new light—as either an opportunity for growth or as a part of what makes you a unique but relatable person?

Take five slow, deep breaths. Reflect in gratitude.

Date: ___/___

Three things I'm grateful for today:

1. _____

_____

2. _____

_____

3. _____

_____

Today I'll express my gratitude to:

Take five slow, deep breaths. Inhale and exhale in gratitude.

Three small moments of joy I experienced today:

1. _____

_____

2. _____

_____

3. _____

_____

Tomorrow I'll do my best to:

Take five slow, deep breaths. Reflect in gratitude.

Date: _____ / _____

Three things I'm grateful for today:

1. _____

_____

2. _____

_____

3. _____

_____

Today I'll express my gratitude to:

Take five slow, deep breaths. Inhale and exhale in gratitude.

Three small moments of joy I experienced today:

1. _____

_____

2. _____

_____

3. _____

_____

Tomorrow I'll do my best to:

Take five slow, deep breaths. Reflect in gratitude.

Date: ___/___

Three things I'm grateful for today:

1. _____

_____

2. _____

_____

3. _____

_____

Today I'll express my gratitude to:

Take five slow, deep breaths. Inhale and exhale in gratitude.

Three small moments of joy I experienced today:

1. _____

_____

2. _____

_____

3. _____

_____

Tomorrow I'll do my best to:

Take five slow, deep breaths. Reflect in gratitude.

Date: ____ / ____

Three things I'm grateful for today:

1. _____

_____

2. _____

_____

3. _____

_____

Today I'll express my gratitude to:

Take five slow, deep breaths. Inhale and exhale in gratitude.

Three small moments of joy I experienced today:

1. _____

_____

2. _____

_____

3. _____

_____

Tomorrow I'll do my best to:

Take five slow, deep breaths. Reflect in gratitude.

Date: ____ / ____

Three things I'm grateful for today:

1. _____

_____

2. _____

_____

3. _____

_____

Today I'll express my gratitude to:

Take five slow, deep breaths. Inhale and exhale in gratitude.

Three small moments of joy I experienced today:

1. _____

_____

2. _____

_____

3. _____

_____

Tomorrow I'll do my best to:

Take five slow, deep breaths. Reflect in gratitude.

Date: ____ / ____

Three things I'm grateful for today:

1. _____

_____

2. _____

_____

3. _____

_____

Today I'll express my gratitude to:

Take five slow, deep breaths. Inhale and exhale in gratitude.

Three small moments of joy I experienced today:

1. _____

_____

2. _____

_____

3. _____

_____

Tomorrow I'll do my best to:

Take five slow, deep breaths. Reflect in gratitude.

Date: ____ / ____

Three things I'm grateful for today:

1. _____

_____

2. _____

_____

3. _____

_____

Today I'll express my gratitude to:

Take five slow, deep breaths. Inhale and exhale in gratitude.

Three small moments of joy I experienced today:

1. _____

_____

2. _____

_____

3. _____

_____

Tomorrow I'll do my best to:

Take five slow, deep breaths. Reflect in gratitude.

One of the most beautiful things about gratitude is just how malleable it is. How many forms it can take. How infinite it feels. Even in those moments when we feel boxed in, gratitude has a way of creating space, understanding, and kindness not just for yourself, but for the communities around you.

Like self-love, a gratitude practice is a life-long process—an act that requires, in truth, one secret ingredient: connection. Think of the names you wrote down, the things you love and appreciate, the moments that made you feel safe and lovely and full of hope. Think of the infinite ways these brave decisions to work toward gratitude have been filled with acceptance, humility, empathy, peace, love, and power. How uniquely *you* those decisions have been. Because at the end of the day, your journey toward gratitude isn't anyone else's. It's yours.

Start an endless loop of gratitude...

Reflect on a time someone expressed gratitude to you. Write a note to them about how meaningful that moment was for you.

Take five slow, deep breaths. Reflect in gratitude.

Date: ___/___

Three things I'm grateful for today:

1. _____

_____

2. _____

_____

3. _____

_____

Today I'll express my gratitude to:

Take five slow, deep breaths. Inhale and exhale in gratitude.

Three small moments of joy I experienced today:

1. _____

_____

2. _____

_____

3. _____

_____

Tomorrow I'll do my best to:

Take five slow, deep breaths. Reflect in gratitude.

Date: _____ / _____

Three things I'm grateful for today:

1. _____

_____

2. _____

_____

3. _____

_____

Today I'll express my gratitude to:

Take five slow, deep breaths. Inhale and exhale in gratitude.

Three small moments of joy I experienced today:

1. _____

_____

2. _____

_____

3. _____

_____

Tomorrow I'll do my best to:

Take five slow, deep breaths. Reflect in gratitude.

Date: ____ / ____

Three things I'm grateful for today:

1. _____

_____

2. _____

_____

3. _____

_____

Today I'll express my gratitude to:

Take five slow, deep breaths. Inhale and exhale in gratitude.

Three things I've learned through my gratitude practice:

1. _____

_____

2. _____

_____

3. _____

_____

From now on, I'll do my best to:

Take five slow, deep breaths. Reflect on everything you've learned in your journey toward gratitude and how much joy and kindness you've already spread through the world!

I'm grateful for you!

There's a lot in my life that I'm grateful for, but one of the things that's brought me the most joy over the course of my life and career is feeling a real connection to people all over the world through my art. I know it probably feels a little one-sided right now, because you know more about me than I know about you, but I swear, the thing that motivates me most as I make projects like this journal—or write books like *Tomorrow I'll Be Brave* and *Tomorrow I'll Be Kind*—is picturing you here, book in hand, experiencing it.

So thank you! Thank you for being "here" with me in the pre-dawn hours (the only time of day I can manage to write) and for being my muse. Thank you for letting me be a part of your life through your gratitude practice. I hope it's been as fulfilling for you to undertake as it's been for me. If you ever want to get in touch and complete our circle of friendship, I'm pretty easy to find on the internet. I do my best to read every email and DM.

I wish you all the best as you keep this awesome, life-changing practice going and look forward to "meeting" again in one of my future projects!

With immense gratitude,

This journal is dedicated, as always, to
my husband, Russ, and kids—Ramona,
Charlie, and George. You all make me feel
pinch-myself grateful every single day.

PENGUIN WORKSHOP
An imprint of Penguin Random House LLC, New York

First published in the United States of America by Penguin Workshop,
an imprint of Penguin Random House LLC, New York, 2021

Visit us online at penguinrandomhouse.com.

Manufactured in China

ISBN 9780593384893   10 9 8 7 6 5 4 3 2 1 TPLF